GUARDING
FORT KNOX

BY LINDA CERNAK

Published by The Child's World®
1980 Lookout Drive • Mankato, MN 56003-1705
800-599-READ • www.childsworld.com

Acknowledgments
The Child's World®: Mary Swensen, Publishing Director
Red Line Editorial: Editorial direction and production
The Design Lab: Design

Design Element: Iaroslav Neliubov/Shutterstock Images
Photographs ©: Bettmann/Corbis, cover, 1; AP Images, 5, 6, 20; Joseph
Sohm/Shutterstock Images, 8; Barry Thumma/AP Images, 10, 12; Patti
Longmire/AP Images, 15; Cliff CC2.0, 16; Everett Historical/Shutterstock
Images, 19

ISBN 9781503808126
LCCN 2015958280

Printed in the United States of America
Mankato, MN
June, 2016
PA02302

ABOUT THE AUTHOR

Linda Cernak is an independent writer of children's classroom readers, student textbooks, and nonfiction books for young readers. Since 1994, she has published numerous children's books in the subject areas of social studies, science, and the arts. Her list of published works also includes a series of fiction readers for elementary-grade students.

TABLE OF CONTENTS

CHAPTER 1

A Storehouse for Gold 4

CHAPTER 2

Inside the Fortress 9

CHAPTER 3

Securing the Fort 14

CHAPTER 4

Gold and Other Treasures 18

GLOSSARY 22

TO LEARN MORE 23

INDEX 24

A Storehouse for Gold

People use gold in different ways. Gold can be a symbol of wealth. Coins and jewelry are made from the metal. Gold can also be a symbol of great achievement. Olympic champions are awarded gold medals.

Gold has been one of the world's most precious metals for thousands of years. Gold was found in California in the 1840s. Settlers traveled thousands of miles to pan for it there. They wanted to get rich. Gold's popularity is still sky-high.

Today, a giant storehouse contains most of the United States' gold. It is called the United States **Bullion Depository**. It is also known as Fort Knox. That is because it is located in Fort Knox, Kentucky. Here, gold is stored in a bar form known as bullion. Each bar is about the size of a brick.

It cost $560,000 to build Fort Knox.

Up until the 1930s, many people had gold coins and bullion. That changed in 1933. President Franklin D. Roosevelt issued an order that year. People had to turn their gold in to the banks. They were allowed to keep their gold jewelry. The gold

A truck unloads gold at Fort Knox in 1940.

was exchanged for U.S. **currency**, or dollars. People were paid about $20 per ounce of gold. The gold coins were melted down. Then they were made into bullion.

The U.S. government needed a place to store all the bullion. So the Treasury Department built a giant depository. The depository had to be big enough to store all the gold. And it had to be secure enough to prevent a break-in.

A site at Fort Knox was chosen. The site was far away from the ocean. This would prevent people launching an attack from the sea. The site was also protected by the Appalachian Mountains. The depository was finished in 1936.

In January 1937, the government began to transfer gold to the depository. The gold was packed into boxes. It was too heavy to fly on an airplane. So, the boxes were loaded onto a train. Then the gold was put into trucks. Police escorts rode beside the trucks as they traveled.

The gold was then loaded onto railroad cars. It took more than 500 railroad cars to carry the gold to Fort Knox. Special agents guarded the

U.S. MINT

Currency in the United States features coins. These coins are made by the U.S. Mint. There are four Mint locations that make coins. They are in San Francisco, Philadelphia, Denver, and West Point, New York. The Mint is part of the U.S. Treasury. Before Fort Knox opened, gold was stored at the mints.

The U.S. Mint in Philadelphia was the country's first.

railroad cars. Finally, the gold was safely stored at the depository.

Never had so much gold been in one place at the same time. That is why Fort Knox had to be one of the most secure buildings in the United States. It is still considered that today.

Inside the Fortress

Want to visit Fort Knox? Not so fast. You would not be able to get near the depository. No visitors are allowed. This is a strict rule with no exceptions. Today, even the U.S. president cannot get into Fort Knox. And no one has ever broken into the building. That is because of all the incredible security measures in place.

Fort Knox is a fortress. It is made up of tons of granite, concrete, and steel. The base of the building is made of layers of cement. Ten feet (3 m) of granite lie on top of the cement. This granite supports the weight of the building and its gold. The thickness of the base makes it pretty much impossible to dig a tunnel to the gold.

The Mint Police guard the depository and its gold. They also protect the four Mint buildings. The Mint Police are highly trained and carry weapons. There is a firing range in the basement of the depository.

A photo of the bullion in Fort Knox taken in 1974, the
last time reporters were let into the vault

Here, members of the Mint Police can practice their
shooting skills. If a person comes too close to the
depository, he or she can be arrested. Don't try to
take a picture with a camera, either. The guards will
take the camera away.

Within the building is a two-story **vault**. This is the
room in which the gold is kept. The vault's concrete
walls are 21 inches (53 cm) thick. They are lined

with steel plates and beams. The vault is divided into compartments. These compartments contain the gold.

The vault has a huge door. It weighs more than 40,000 pounds (18,144 kg). It is made of blast-proof materials. The door is also drill-proof and fireproof. Offices and storerooms surround the vault. Beyond these are the outer walls of the building. These walls are made of granite. They are lined with cement, steel, and fireproof materials.

The vault has other special security features. It is set on a timer. The door can only be opened every 104 hours. If a person accidentally becomes locked inside the vault, there is an escape route. A narrow tunnel leads out of the vault. A person must crawl through it to escape. At the end is a door that can only be opened from inside the tunnel. The door leads to the outside of the vault. But it does not lead to the outside of the depository.

So, who gets into the vault? The answer is, nearly nobody. Even some presidents have been denied

Mint director Mary Brooks leads reporters and members
of Congress during their 1974 tour of Fort Knox.

access. The only president to visit the vault was
Franklin D. Roosevelt. That was in 1943.

The last time outsiders were allowed into the vault
was 1974. People began to wonder about all the
security. Why was no one allowed in the vault? They
wondered if gold was even in the depository. Some

people thought the vault was empty. Others thought powerful people were secretly removing the gold.

So the U.S. Treasury decided to allow outside visitors. Members of Congress were chosen to enter the vault. About 120 reporters were also allowed entry. It was an exciting event. The vault doors were finally opened. The visitors entered in small groups. They saw the gold compartments. No other outsiders have been allowed in since.

Each compartment was sealed with special tape. The tape ensured that the compartments had remained sealed. Bulbs from the reporters' cameras flashed. It made the gold glitter. Mary Brooks was the Mint director at the time. "I'm very happy to show the country that the gold is here," she said.

THE SECRET COMBINATION

The vault can only be opened with a secret combination. The series of numbers for the vault is well guarded. No one person knows the entire combination. Several people must dial separate sequences to open the door. The combinations to the vault change daily.

CHAPTER 3

Securing the Fort

The gold in Fort Knox is worth billions of dollars. Such a valuable resource needs to be protected. That is why the depository is located near an army base. Here, soldiers are trained for the U.S. Army. If there was an attack on the depository, troops would be ready. Tanks and attack helicopters are on call for protection. So are powerful **artillery** weapons.

At the depository, guards use high-tech equipment to watch the entire complex. Much of the technology is top secret. Different **surveillance** tools view every inch of Fort Knox. There are video cameras and microphones throughout the building. And there are alarms everywhere. Windows are made of bulletproof glass. They are darkened so nobody can get a good look at what is inside.

Fort Knox is home to both a gold
depository and a military base.

There are two **sentry** boxes at the entry gate of
Fort Knox. These are lookout boxes. Guards are
posted here. Inside the gates are four more guard
boxes at the corners of the building. Here, members
of the Mint Police are on watch at all hours.

Fences surround the depository. The first fence
was built in 1936. It is shaped like an octagon.

PROTECTING THE FORT

cameras

guards

cement wall

sentry box

fence

Two more electric fences were later built. They surround the inner fence. Guards patrol the area between the fences.

Beyond the electric fences is a wide-open area. This lets guards spot an intruder trying to sneak up to the building. Beyond the open area is a barbed wire fence. This fence encloses the entire complex.

It is the first line of defense against people trying to sneak into one of the most secure buildings in the world.

Outside fences are equipped with special night-vision cameras.

NIGHT-VISION CAMERAS

Night-vision cameras work in two ways. The camera can increase dim light at nighttime. This is light that comes from the Moon or stars. Or, a night-vision camera can pick up light that humans cannot see. This is known as infrared light.

There are microphones everywhere, too. If an intruder manages to climb over a fence, floodlights will turn on. Booming alarms will ring. The intruder will not get very far. The Mint Police will likely arrest the person.

Top-secret technology protects the depository. Only a few people know exactly what it is. There might be a satellite defense system. Or there could be land mines between the fences. Perhaps there are hidden missiles or automatic weapons.

Not many people know all the secret ways Fort Knox is guarded. That makes it even more dangerous to try to break into.

CHAPTER 4

Gold and Other Treasures

Today, the U.S. Treasury reports there are about 147 million ounces (4,167,379,899 g) of gold at Fort Knox. Each gold bar weighs about 27 pounds (12 kg). It is hard to estimate how much a gold bar is worth. That is because the price of gold changes. However, the Treasury sets a standard price for gold in the depository. It is about $42 dollars per ounce. So, each gold bar would have a value of about $16,888.

Gold is not the only treasure that has been kept in the vault. Many important items have been stored there. During World War II, Germans were bombing London. Nobody knew what was going to happen. So the British government asked the United States for help. The United States stored some of Great Britain's rare historical papers and priceless jewels

The German bombings of Great Britain caused Europeans to ask the United States to guard important items in Fort Knox during World War II.

in Fort Knox. The U.S. Declaration of Independence and Constitution were also sent there.

There are many **conspiracy** theories about what else might have been hidden in Fort Knox. Conspiracy theories can be connected to secret plots. Or they may involve illegal schemes. In the 1950s, some people believed morphine was stocked in the vault. Morphine is a painkiller. It is often used on a battlefield. It helps ease pain for wounded

The Declaration of Independence was moved to the
National Archives Building, its current home, in 1952.

soldiers. People believed the drug was put in the
vault in case of another war.

Conspiracy theories are still around today. That is
because of the high security surrounding the vault.
It is also because Fort Knox has not been opened
to the public in decades. What could be hidden

there? Some people suspect the vault holds **biological** war weapons. Still others think bodies from outer space are locked away. Some even think there is no gold inside. They think the government has secretly sold it to other countries.

The gold in Fort Knox was counted in 1953. It was counted during an official **audit**. Since then, only partial audits have taken place. So exactly how much gold is in Fort Knox today? What secrets may lie inside? The only way to solve these mysteries is for the vault to be opened and inspected. And that is not likely to happen anytime soon.

TRANSPORTING THE DECLARATION OF INDEPENDENCE AND THE CONSTITUTION

The Declaration of Independence and the Constitution helped build the United States. So they needed to be taken care of during transport. They were wrapped in acid-free paper. Then they were securely locked in a bronze chest. The chest was packed in a box that weighed about 150 pounds (68 kg). An armed truck escorted the box to a railway station. Secret Service and U.S. cavalry troops guarded the truck. The documents stayed at Fort Knox until 1944.

GLOSSARY

artillery (ahr-TIL-uh-ree) Artillery is a collection of large, heavy weapons. A lot of artillery is stored at the military base near Fort Knox.

audit (AW-dit) An audit is an official examination of financial accounts. There was an official audit of the gold in Fort Knox in 1953.

biological (by-uh-LOJ-i-kuhl) A biological weapon is one that uses bacteria or a virus that can hurt living things. Some think dangerous biological war weapons are stored in Fort Knox.

bullion (BOOL-yuhn) Bullion is gold or silver in the form of bars. There are thousands of pounds of bullion inside Fort Knox.

conspiracy (kuhn-SPIR-uh-see) A conspiracy is a secret plot to do something wrong or against the law. There are many conspiracy theories about what is held inside the vault at Fort Knox.

currency (KUR-uhn-see) Currency is something that is used as money such as coins or paper bills. In 1933 people traded in their gold for currency.

depository (dih-PAWZ-i-toh-ree) A depository is a place where something is stored for safekeeping. The vault at Fort Knox is a depository for gold.

sentry (SEN-tree) A sentry is a person stationed at a place to stand guard. A sentry keeps watch in each of the boxes at the entrance of Fort Knox.

surveillance (ser-VEY-luhns) Surveillance is keeping watch over a person, group, or place. Video cameras are used for surveillance at Fort Knox.

vault (VAWLT) A vault is a room built with strong materials for the safekeeping of valuables. The vault at Fort Knox has thick walls and a huge door.

TO LEARN MORE

IN THE LIBRARY

Friedman, Mel. *The California Gold Rush*. New York: Scholastic, 2010.

Furgang, Kathy, and Fred Hiebert. *Everything Money*. Washington, DC: National Geographic, 2013.

Lange, David W. *History of the United States Mint and its Coinage*. Atlanta: Whitman Publishing, 2006.

ON THE WEB

Visit our Web site for links about guarding
Fort Knox: **childsworld.com/links**

*Note to Parents, Teachers, and Librarians: We routinely verify
our Web links to make sure they are safe and active sites.
So encourage your readers to check them out!*

INDEX

Appalachian Mountains, 7

Brooks, Mary, 13

California, 4
combinations, 13
conspiracies, 19–21

Denver, 7

Kentucky, 4

London, 18

Mint Police, 9–10, 15, 17

Philadelphia, 7

Roosevelt, Franklin D., 5, 12

San Francisco, 7
Secret Service, 21
settlers, 4

tunnel, 9, 11

U.S. Army, 14
U.S. Constitution, 19, 21
U.S. Declaration of
   Independence, 19, 21
U.S. Mint, 7, 9
U.S. Treasury Department, 6, 7,
   13, 18

vault, 10–13, 18–21

West Point, 7
World War II, 18